T0004263

LUKE JOHN MATTHEW ARNOLD

NOBODY REALLY HAS THEIR SHIT TOGETHER

DOODLES TO MAKE YOU FEEL KIND OF BETTER

Hardie Grant

BOOKS

I want to acknowledge the Traditional Owners of the land on which I create, the Walbanga People of the Yuin Nation, and pay my respects to Elders past, present and emerging. Sovereignty was never ceded and this Country always was and always will be Aboriginal and Torres Strait Islander land.

To Jessica,
thanks for teaching this
dickhead what kindness
and friendship really is.
I bloody love ya!

For most of us, every day comes with a new set of 'holy shits' and 'what the fucks'. But as a fella who lives with OCD and anxiety while also being an artist, it's safe to say I can't often afford a shrink. I've meditated (aka: napped) and I've also tried writing a daily diary – but I'd always hear myself in my head as an English maiden, mourning the loss of her beloved at sea. His name was Arthur, but I called him Artie. Surprisingly, this didn't help much.

So I started doodling. Doodling cute images that hugged my eyeballs and kissed my heart with sassy words that spanked my 'negative thinking' on the big ol' bum.

These doodles, as absurd as many (most) are, have helped me traverse the deepest of shit puddles and come out the other side – moist and smelly but okay. I am hoping that the little bit of magic that's gotten me through will rub off on you. I want these doodles to be able to make you feel

less like shit – to feel like sharing
a beer with a mate rather than
sleeping all day, or just having a cup
of tea and watching the telly if you need.

All in all, this book is here for you to whip
out and open at any page, anytime with
the comfort of knowing that whatever
doodle you look at is totally cheese-free,
bullshit-free and has worked to cheer one
person up. Hopefully you're number two.

PS: As you flip through the book,
you will come across little activities
you might want to do or share with
mates – and yay, that's great! However – and
I don't want to get all bossy bitch on you – but
maybe scan and print the pages and don't
approach the book like a rabid honey
badger to a cobra ... Why? 'Cos if you
copy them, you can do them again and
again and again ... Oh, the repetitive joy!

Luke x

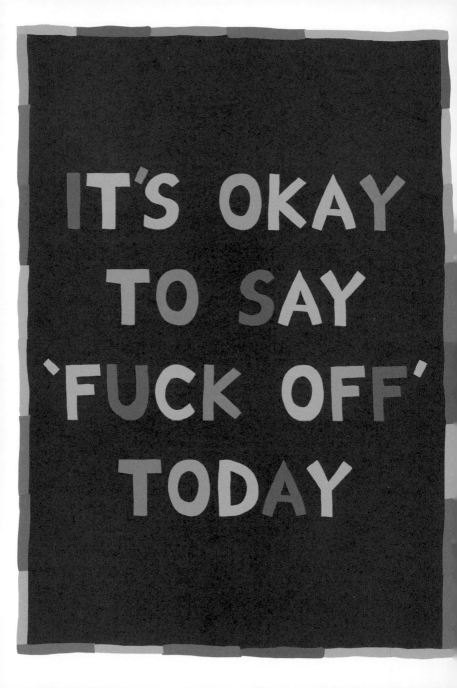

IS LIKE A CROCODILE,
IT CREEPS BELOW THE
SURFACE FOR A WHILE.

WITH NO WARNING
THERE COMES A SNAP
AND YOU'RE RANTING
ABOUT BEING OVER
THIS CRAP.

BITTEN OFF MORE
THAN YOU CAN CHEW?
JUST SWALLOW
FOR TOMORROW

IT
WILL
JUST
BE POO.

I
OFTEN
SEE DRAGONS

I ALWAYS SEE SHEEP

AND USUALLY
I FALL

RIGHT
THE FUCK
TO SLEEP

SELF
LOVE
SPELL

THIS SPELL ISN'T FOR
THE FAINT OF HEART
NOR FOR THOSE
WHO HAVE TO BE UP
EARLY TOMORROW
MORNING FOR ANY
FORM OF WORK.

WHAT YOU'LL NEED

cauldron (aka: large pot, salad bowl, bucket)

ladle & jar

bottle of spirits destined to be released (spirits of choice: gin, vodka, tequila)

bottle of bubbles

bottle of dead fruits' blood (aka: tropical fruit juice)

can of dead fruits' flesh (your choice of victim)

bottle of a lemon's hopes and joys (aka: lemonade)

2 large pizzas and a garlic bread, summoned

a bingeworthy series frozen in time, awaiting your powerful finger to free it

STEPS

1. Combine ingredients 3–7 in your cauldron.

2. Stir with ladle, sip to taste, and when perfect, let out a loud cackle (to warn the neighbours it's going to be one of 'those nights').

3. Place cauldron between yourself and the television. It is important that you can replenish your jar without having to leave the lounge.

4. On either side of your cauldron, place one large pizza. Now raise the garlic bread above your head to mother moon and repeat this incantation three times:

'I AM AMAZING, I AM GREAT, I AM IN CHARGE OF MY OWN FUCKING FATE.

I AM MAGICAL, I AM DAMN FINE, I AM READY FOR SOME LOVING ME TIME.'

5. Yas, you bad witch! Now free that bingeworthy series with a touch of your magical finger.

6. Sit back, revel in your own company, ingest your potion and food from the goddesses ravishingly and responsibly.

DON'T LET
FUCKING UP
GET YOU DOWN.
IT'S HELPING
YOU FIND A
NEW WAY
AROUND.

THESE ARE SOME THINGS THAT YOU CAN DO TO HELP A FRIEND WHO IS FEELING BLUE:

- SEND SOME LOVE IN THE FORM OF A RHYME

- CALL – DON'T TEXT – AND ENJOY TALK TIME

- CUDDLE AND KISS IF THAT'S YOUR THING

- BEAD THEM A BRACELET OR DODGY-ASS RING

- SEND CONSENSUAL NUDES, IF THEY LIKE WHAT YOU'VE GOT

- TAKE OVER SOME SNACKS AND PERHAPS SOME POT

- PICK PRETTY FLOWERS FROM NEXT DOOR

- CHECK IN WITH THEM AND LISTEN SOME MORE

HORNINESS

IS A HOPPY LITTLE
RABBIT. CUTE AS A
BUTTON, WITH A REAL
FUCK-HABIT.

MAKING LOVE AND
MANY A BABY, THEIR
LITTLE NOSE WIGGLE
IS SAYING
'JUST LAY ME.'

BATSHIT CRAY AND A-OK

DEAR ME,

This feels like a catastrophe, but please don't forget it's also temporary.

So, I'm sending this to future you, who will look back and say you knew that I am: strong, tough and will get through ...

And I am and I did and I am here thanks to you.

BIG LOVE,

xxx

JUST KEEP
IT UP
KEEP IT
GOING
MAKE
MISTAKES
TO KEEP IT
FLOWING

THESE ARE SOME THINGS I DO WHEN I'M NOT HAPPY TO MAKE MYSELF FEEL LESS THAN CRAPPY

- TOUCH A TREE WITH YOUR HAND. YOU CAN SAY HELLO BUT IT WON'T UNDERSTAND

- PAT A DOG FOR AN HOUR, THEY HAVE A SOUL-SLOBBERING SUPERPOWER

- TAKE A WALK DOWN THE STREET AND UBER BACK TO REWARD YOUR FEAT

- HAVE A JOINT OR BAKE A BROWNIE BUT NIBBLE AWAY OR YOU MAY GET FROWNY

- HAVE A BATH AND TOUCH YOURSELF, USE THE OLD BATHBOMB ON THE TOP SHELF

- SIT AT A PARK AND SAY 'HEY' TO EVERYONE, STATISTICALLY YOU SHOULD MEET SOMEONE FUN

- TELL YASELF THAT FEELING CRAPPY IS TOTALLY FINE AND BEING HAPPY WILL COME IN GOOD TIME

LIFE CAN SUCK AND BE TOTALLY TRAGIC,

BUT THEN LIFE CAN FLIP AND BE FUCKING MAGIC!

LIKES AIN'T LOVE

SHAKE OFF THE SHIT. RINSE OFF THE GLOOM. DUST OFF YOUR SOUL. JUST FUCKING BLOOM.

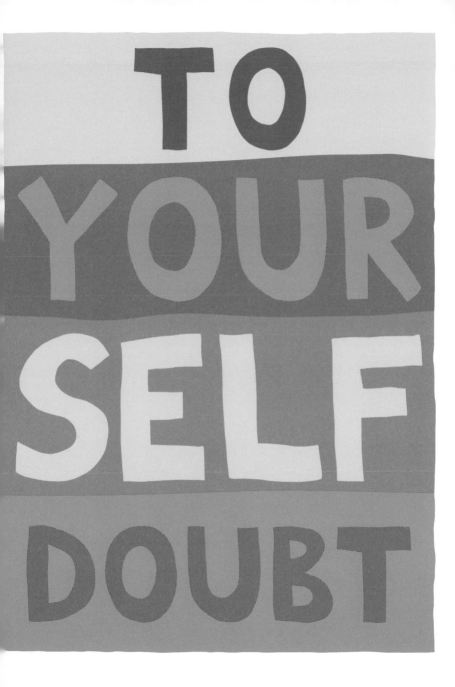

TO YOUR SELF DOUBT

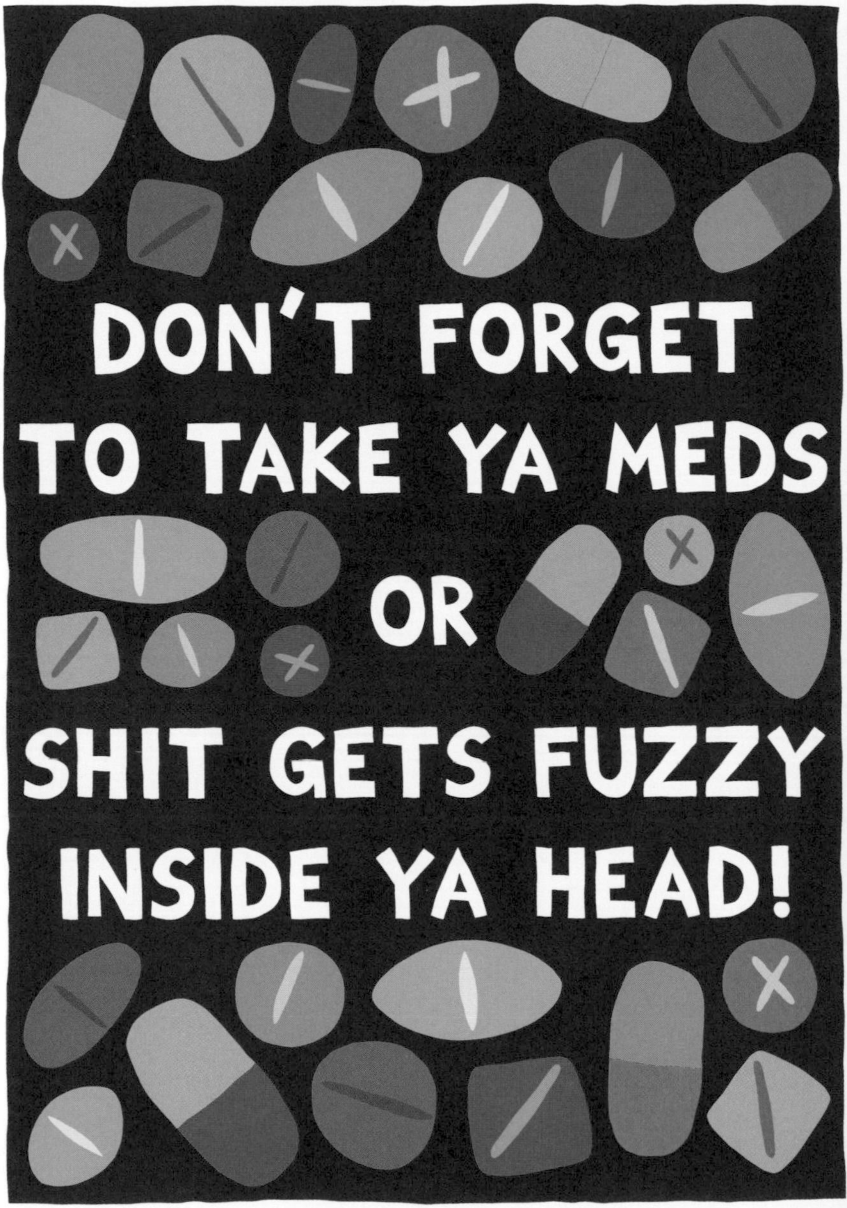
DON'T FORGET
TO TAKE YA MEDS
OR
SHIT GETS FUZZY
INSIDE YA HEAD!

DEAR _____

I wanted to send you this note to say a huge THANK YOU for:

- [ ] Being the best friend ever
- [ ] Being the best friend with benefits ever
- [ ] Talking me out of getting a pet gecko
- [ ] Seeing if I'm okay, when you know I fucking ain't
- [ ] Lip syncing 'All By Myself' to defrost my cold, dead heart
- [ ] _____

I am so lucky to have you in my world!

LOVE _____

BEING A DICK TODAY DOESN'T MEAN YOU HAVE TO BE A DICK TOMORROW

YOU'RE DOING GREAT
YOU'RE GOING WELL
EVEN WHEN YA NOT...
COZ THIS FUCKING
WORLD IS HARD
AS SHIT
AND JUST 'BEING'
IS A LOT.

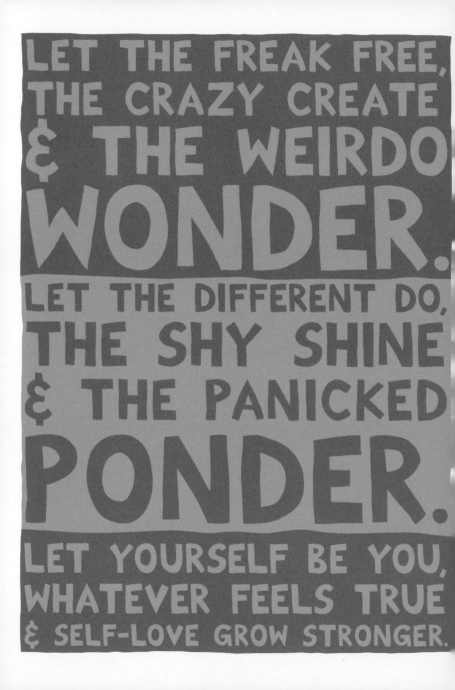

'PICK YA FUCKING BATTLES,'
THEY ALWAYS SAY.

I'D RATHER PICK FLOWERS
& HAND SOME YOUR WAY.

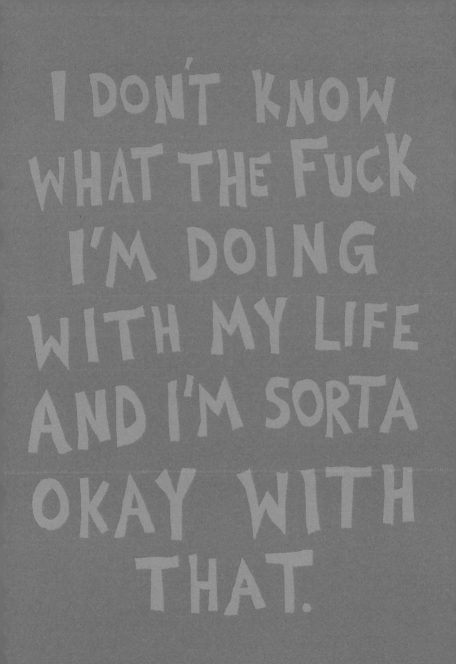

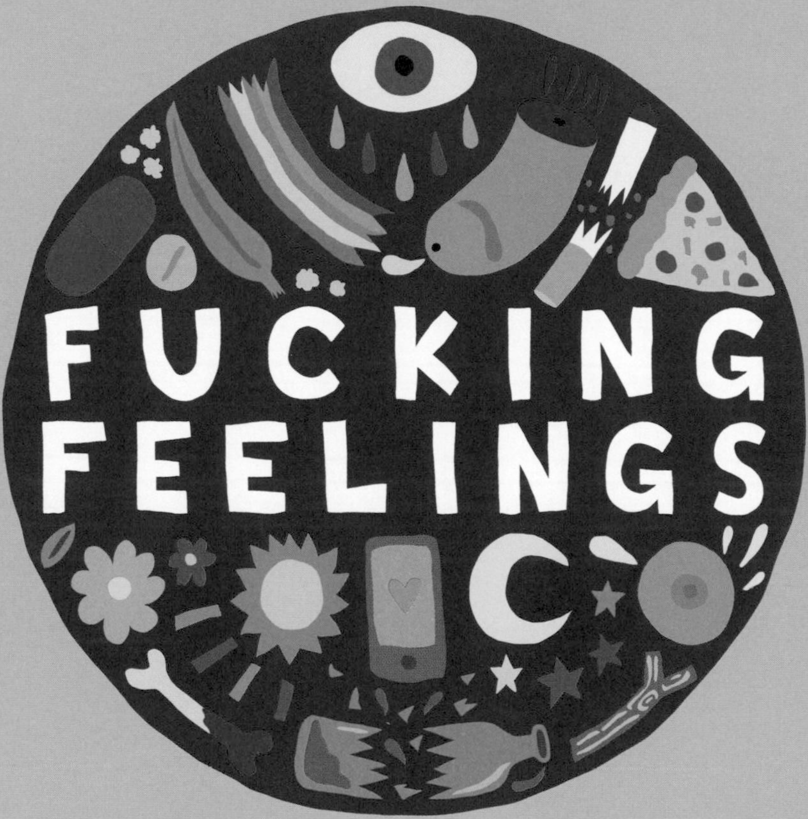
FUCKING
FEELINGS

HAPPINESS

IS A DOLPHIN FREE,
BLOWING FROM HOLES
AND SLAYING THE SEA.

THEY SMILE AND SING
AS THEY SWIM
TOGETHER IN AN
OCEANIC PARTY THAT
GOES ON FOREVER.

BE PROUD
BE HAPPY
WHEN YOU MOVE
THE FUCK ON
FROM SOMETHING
CRAPPY

FILL YOUR

HEART UP!

Copy and print both of these pages.
Cut and paste on your heart.
Fill in two simple stages!

ANXIOUS AND BRAVE AS FUCK

THAT SHADE OF CONFIDENCE LOOKS HOT AS FUCK ON YOU

EVIL

IS A CAT SO FLUFFY
CLAWING YOUR FLESH
AND YOUR EYES NOW
PUFFY.

THEY LURE YOU IN
WITH PURRS OF LOVE,
BUT APPROACH WITH
CAUTION, A FACE SHIELD
AND GLOVES.

I'VE LOST
MY KEYS, PHONE
AND DRUNKEN
WAY HOME.
MY VIRGINITY,
SANITY AND
SELF-LOATHING
VANITY.
SOME FRIENDS,
MORE FOES, AND
FUCK ONLY KNOWS
THE COOL SHIT I'LL
FIND TOMORROW!

YOU CAN DREAM BIG OR YOU CAN DREAM SMALL, PERHAPS YOU DREAM NOTHING AND ARE BLESSED WITH IT ALL.

YOUR DREAMS MAY
BE FAR OR
SOON TO COME TRUE,
BUT WHATEVER YOUR
DREAMS
BE SURE THEY'RE FOR
YOU.

AGAIN SOON...

TOMORROW
BRINGS
WHAT TODAY
COULD NOT

HOW TO KNOW IF A PERSON IS GOOD FOR YOUR SOUL OR A BAD ASSHOLE

- IF THEY DON'T LIKE ANY SORT OF CHEESE, BACK AWAY, CALL AN UBER PLEASE

- IF THEY TALK TO ANIMALS AND PRETEND THEY REPLY, THIS IS A GOOD PERSON AND GIVE THEM A TRY

- IF THEY POO ON YOUR WINS AND REJOICE WHEN YOU FAIL, SHOW THEM THE WHARF, IT'S TIME THEY SET SAIL

- IF THEY ARE KIND AND SPEW LOVE EVERYWHERE, THROW SLUMBER PARTIES AND PLAIT EACH OTHER'S HAIR

- IF THEY DON'T THINK INCLUSIVITY IS A THING, HANG UP ON THEM AND GIVE YOUR NANNA A RING

- IF THEY MAKE YOU LAUGH SO HARD YOU LEAK SOME PEE, IT'S TIME YOU ADD THEM TO YOUR FAMILY TREE

UNSETTLE

PETAL

Certificate of

F♥CKING AWESOMENESS

Awarded to:

For:

From:

LOVE YOUR BEAUTIFUL MAGICAL FUCKING SELF

LUKE JOHN MATTHEW ARNOLD

is a name hog, visual artist and illustrator working on Yuin Country in Braidwood. Using text, pop colours and balanced motifs, Luke finds inspiration in everyday (crass) communications. He also creates work that pushes for equality and inclusivity for the LGBTQIA+ community as well as (over)sharing his mental health journey in the hope of breaking down the stigma and encouraging others to feel comfortable to join the conversation. Luke has developed creative workshops and programs for marginalised communities for the past decade and now works as a lecturer in visual arts. He collaborates with international brands and campaigns, and continues to share his work on Instagram.

SUPPORT

Mental health and life in general can be a genuine pain in the dick at times and if you feel you need some professional support, here are some numbers that may be helpful:

Australia
Lifeline: 13 11 14

UK
Campaign Against Living Miserably: 0800 58 58 58

US
988 Suicide & Crisis Lifeline: 988

THANK YOU

Mum, thanks for often being my muse for many of the crass phrases – we have refined potty-mouths. Your love is just like your laugh: loud and unescapable. I love you.

Dad, thanks for always having my back. I'll always get you a 'claw' when wanted. Love you and Kathi lots.

Adam, you walked with me through all of these artworks, existing in the harder reality of them. Thank you for making me see that my mental health isn't who I am and that I can do whatever I put my mind, pencil and page to. Massive love and BK x.

Vlad, you were there from the very start, when I doodled my first doodle. You also gave me the greatest piece of advice: 'fake your way to success'. Thank you, cuzzy.

Berry, you can't read because you're a dog, so I will interpret this via peanut butter-covered biscuits and shameful baby talk. You are always the happiest presence in my life and I swear I wouldn't be here if it weren't for you. Thanks for being the coolest bitch in town.

Published in 2023 by Hardie Grant Books, an imprint of Hardie Grant Publishing

Hardie Grant Books (Melbourne)
Wurundjeri Country
Building 1, 658 Church Street
Richmond, Victoria 3121

Hardie Grant Books (London)
5th & 6th Floors
52–54 Southwark Street
London SE1 1UN

hardiegrant.com/books

Hardie Grant acknowledges the Traditional Owners of the Country on which we
work, the Wurundjeri People of the Kulin Nation and the Gadigal People of the
Eora Nation, and recognises their continuing connection to the land, waters
and culture. We pay our respects to their Elders past and present.

All rights reserved. No part of this publication may be reproduced, stored in a retrieval system
or transmitted in any form by any means, electronic, mechanical, photocopying, recording
or otherwise, without the prior written permission of the publishers and copyright holders.

The moral rights of the author have been asserted.

Copyright text and illustration © Luke John Matthew Arnold 2023
Copyright design © Hardie Grant Publishing 2023

A catalogue record for this
book is available from the
National Library of Australia

Nobody Really Has Their Sh*t Together
ISBN 978 1 74379 995 6

10 9 8 7 6 5 4 3 2 1

Design by Amy Daoud
Author photo by Rocket K. Weijers
Printed in China by Leo Paper Products LTD.

The paper this book is printed on is from FSC®-certified forests and other
sources. FSC® promotes environmentally responsible, socially beneficial
and economically viable management of the world's forests.